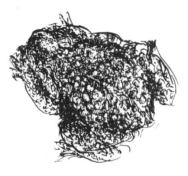

CANE
TOADS
An Unnatural History

Based on the film
Cane Toads: An Unnatural History,
written and directed by Mark Lewis

DOLPHIN/DOUBLEDAY
New York London Toronto Sydney Auckland

C·A·N·E TOADS

An Unnatural History

STEPHANIE LEWIS

Illustrations by Madeline Sorel

A DOLPHIN BOOK
PUBLISHED BY DOUBLEDAY
a division of Bantam Doubleday Dell Publishing Group, Inc.
666 Fifth Avenue, New York, New York 10103

DOLPHIN, DOUBLEDAY and the portrayal of two
dolphins are trademarks of Doubleday, a division of
Bantam Doubleday Dell Publishing Group, Inc.

Library of Congress Cataloging-in-Publication Data
Lewis, Stephanie.
    Cane toads : an unnatural history / by Stephanie
    Lewis. — 1st ed.
    p.   cm.
    1. Cane toad.   I. Title.
QL668.E227L49   1989
597.8′7—dc20   89-7759

ISBN 0-385-26502-6

This book is dedicated to my son Mark,
who became intrigued with the cane
toad story many years ago

We thank the many people who shared
their experiences and their knowledge
with us.

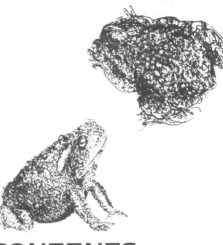

CONTENTS

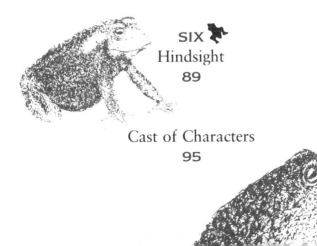

Photo Credits

Page 1: Photo courtesy of Arthur Mostead. Page 5: Photo courtesy of Tip Byrne. Page 9: Photo courtesy of Mark Lewis, *Cane Toads*. Page 24: Photo courtesy of the Linnean Society of New South Wales. Page 26: Courtesy of *The Bulletin*. Page 32: Photo courtesy of Arthur Mostead. Page 34: Courtesy of Queensland Museum. Page 34: Courtesy of Mark Lewis, *Cane Toads*. Page 36: Courtesy of Mark Lewis, *Cane Toads*. Page 38: Courtesy of Jim Frazier, Densey Clyne, Mantis Wildlife Films. Page 40: Courtesy of Mark Lewis, *Cane Toads*. Page 41: Courtesy of Jim Frazier, Densey Clyne, Mantis Wildlife Films. Page 42: Courtesy of Jim Frazier, Densey Clyne, Mantis Wildlife Films. Page 44: Courtesy of *Townsville Bulletin*. Page 45: Courtesy of *Townsville Bulletin*. Page 49: Courtesy of Matt Mawson and the *Cane Toad Times*. Page 54: Courtesy of Patrick Cook. Page 56: Courtesy of David Sondergard. Page 57: Courtesy of Rhyl Yates. Page 58: Courtesy of Chris Higgins and *Quest Community Newspapers*. Page 59: Courtesy of Mark Lewis, *Cane Toads*. Page 60: Courtesy of Mark Lewis, *Cane Toads*. Page 61: Courtesy of Jon Lewis. Page 61: Courtesy of the *Courier-Mail*, 1987. Page 62: Courtesy of Arthur Mostead. Page 62: Courtesy of Jim Frazier, Densey Clyne, Mantis Wildlife Films. Page 62: Courtesy of Arthur Mostead. Page 63: Courtesy of Rhyl Yates. Page 64: Courtesy of Gerry Connolly. Page 67: Courtesy of the *Courier-Mail*. Page 67: Courtesy of David Kapernick. Page 71: Courtesy of Jon Lewis. Page 74: Courtesy of Kaz Cooke. Page 80: Courtesy of Mark Lewis, *Cane Toads*. Page 85: Courtesy of Tip Byrne. Page 92: Courtesy of Matt Mawson and the *Cane Toad Times*. Page 93: Courtesy of Mark Lewis, *Cane Toads*.

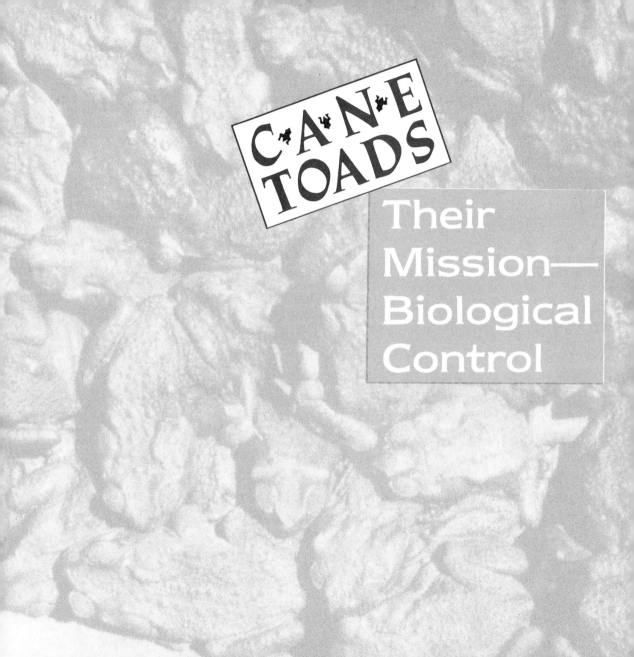

C·A·N·E TOADS

Their Mission— Biological Control

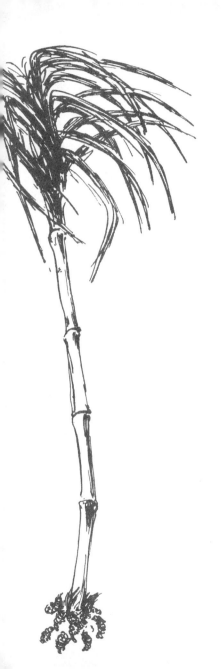

ONE

Everyone knows that sugar is sweet and toads are repulsive, so it's really uncanny how two such seemingly unrelated items came to be lumped together. But so they were. Toads were brought to Australia in 1935 for a specific purpose— to rescue a sugar industry that was in trouble.

In Australia sugarcane grows on the fertile flats along about a thousand kilometres, or six hundred miles, of the East Coast, from the north of New South Wales at the Clarence River up the Queensland coast clear to Mossman, its far northern outpost. It's a major export and a mighty industry.

A field of sugarcane is a glorious sight. The emerald-green stalks grow as thick as five centimetres (two inches) around and more than twice the height of a man. This is the cane derived from the species *Saccharum officinarum,* or "sugar of the apothecaries," and its soft, sweet, juicy stalks have earned it the reputation of being the "noble" cane.[1] But despite nobility, it still has a tendency to fall flat on its face. Then, the emerald fields, so bright in the Queensland sunshine, change their dress to desert brown. The beetle has struck.[*]

Growing sugarcane has never been an easy game: it has been constant warfare with the beetles. The beetles are native to Australia; they existed first, before the sugar plantations.[2] The beetles used to stick to the leaves of the trees in the forests, the same forests out of which the plantations were carved. When the cane was planted, the beetles

---

[1] S. W. Mintz, *Sweetness and Power: The Place of Sugar in Modern History* (New York: Viking Penguin, 1985), p. 21.

---

[*] *Actually, there are two species of beetles—the Greyback and the Frenchi—whose grubs attack the sugar cane. Both are equally resilient and equally pestilent and roughly look about the same. They are between 2.5 and 5 centimetres (one to two inches) long, with horny forewings that cover and protect the hind wings, and their legs look like fretwork saw blades.*

---

[2] Raphael Cilento, *Triumph in the Tropics* (Brisbane: Smith and Patterson, 1959), p. 295.

found the leaves of the cane as much to their liking as those of the weeping fig tree and they'd drop their eggs onto the ground around the cane plants. The eggs became grubs that migrated until they found the roots of the cane upon which they chewed. Then, when there was a bit of a blow or some rain, the stalks, weakened by the loss of their anchor to the nourishing soil, would wilt and collapse.

There was no known way then to control the beetles or the grubs and the problem propagated itself. The more beetles, the more grubs—breeding and multiplying—until the 1930s when they peaked. The cane growers, victims of the pest, were desperate.

A steady campaign was being waged against the beetles by the Bureau of Sugar Experiment Stations, with headquarters in Brisbane and stations scattered throughout the cane-growing areas. The Bureau provided advisory services and research laboratories for the sugar industry and was supposed to be able to supply the growers with solutions to their problems, but this one was becoming too hard. It was a dilemma for the industry that became even more drastic in the Depression years, when the price of sugar dropped and every possible method of attack had been tried.

I remember what it was like on my father's small farm. He would cut a thousand ton of cane. Then there'd be a bad attack of grubs and he'd get a hundred ton. You'd be around here, say, February, March, and you'd see all the cane was yellow—paddocks of fifteen, sixteen acres—completely dead.
—TIP BYRNE, cane farmer, Tully

I've had over fifty years' experience growing cane, and I still remember the crisis. We were about at the end of our tether—the farmers goin' broke—the grubs takin' over. The beetles—they flew out in the thousands. You'd travel along the road at night in the car—you were flat out tryin' to see out the windscreen.

—JACK CLARK,
cane farmer, Gordonvale

They'd tried fumigation with carbon disulphide, a poisonous and evil-smelling compound, in knapsacks strapped to a man's back and a hand-held spear to inject the poison into the soil every twenty centimetres (about nine inches). It took a full week for a man to do about a third of an acre in the hottest, most humid time of the year and sickness was rampant. As the old-timers remember, "You couldn't get labour to do the job and you couldn't blame anyone for not wanting to do it."

Another contraption used against the beetle was a mechanical control which took advantage of the phototropic quality of the beetle—its tendency to be attracted to light. The farmers would get a big metal panel—galvanized iron painted white—with a light in the centre of it and a funnel at the bottom leading into a kerosene tin. They'd switch the light on next to a feeding tree—such as the weeping fig. Then they'd shake the tree. Beetles would fly out into the light—hit the panel—and down the chute they'd go—into the kerosene tin.

Only now is it possible to toss it off and concede that these techniques seem more like fun and games for schoolboys rather than a serious threat to the beetles. But at that time it was pretty much all they had.

Different farmers tried different techniques. Some farmers handpicked the beetles off their cane, others used the metal contraptions and still others just prayed for dry spells to trap the grubs in the soil and prevent them from mating. Then, if it rained, one can only imagine the frustration of the growers as they helplessly watched the soil get moist and soft, knowing that the grubs, now developed into beetles, could emerge to breed more of their kind.

Yet into this picture of gloom there came first a mere glimmer and then a brighter gleam of light. In 1932, the International Society of Sugar Cane Technologists held its Fourth Congress in Puerto Rico. The good news for the Bureau was that the Queensland government would send a representative to the Congress—Arthur Bell, pathologist and entomologist and deputy director at Bureau headquarters.

It was at this fateful conference that Raquel Dexter, a leading entomologist of the time, introduced the toad to sugar growers from all over the world. Known then as the "imported toad, *Bufo marinus*," this species lived as a native only in the area which spanned from southern Mexico to northern Argentina.

Raquel Dexter's paper, though academic and

DIFFERENT FARMERS TRIED DIFFERENT TECHNIQUES:
When we were kids, my sisters and I would get up at half past four in the morning to pick the beetles off the cane. The beetle would fly into the cane between four and six in the morning, and as soon as sunrise came, he automatically dropped off and bored his hole into the ground and you'd miss him. We got sixpence a bucket of beetles.
—TIP BYRNE

MEXICO

VENEZUELA

COLUMBIA

GUYANA

ECUADOR

P E R U

B R A Z I L

BOLIVIA

miles

CHILE

ARGENTINA

PARAGUAY

URUGUAY

detailed statistically, was impassioned. Her subject, *Bufo marinus,* imported from Jamaica, had become a local hero in Puerto Rico. Since its introduction in the 1920s, she had been studying its food habits, and her findings, derived from examination of stomach contents, were consolidated into tables that showed the toad to be a predator of the sugarcane beetles. She was completely convinced that the toad was an effective biological control of the beetles and implored her audience to incorporate *Bufo marinus* into their beetle control programmes.

Some of the delegates to the Congress were so impressed that they made immediate arrangements to take consignments of toads from San Juan for the purpose of establishing them as a predator in their own countries. Cyril Pemberton, the executive entomologist of the Hawaiian Sugar Planters Association Experiment Station, arranged for a consignment of toads to be sent to him in Oahu the following month, April 1932. Arthur Bell, Queensland's representative, was more conservative and

The only thing that could control the grub was a bout of *dry* weather. If we got dry periods when the grubs were developed enough to get out of the ground to fly and mate—well then, if the ground wasn't moist, they couldn't get out. We used to pray for dry weather. Druther have drought! We could forgo a crop by drought because then we got relief for two, maybe three years before the beetles could breed up again.

—JACK CLARK

8

didn't work quite that fast. He went home to his administrative job with the Bureau of Sugar Experiment Stations in Brisbane and mulled it over.

Arthur Bell mulled. The farmers clamoured. The beetles mated. The grubs chewed. The cane stalks collapsed. The beetles flew. The farmers wept, swore, and shook their fists. It was cyclical. For a while it went on like that, picking off beetles, setting up light panels, injecting carbon disulphide, praying for dry weather—all the homely things they did with their fingers crossed. It couldn't go on like that forever.

Meanwhile, back in Hawaii, the toad had undergone a slight change in nomenclature. From having been the "imported toad," it became the "Introduced Tropical American Toad." In July 1934, two years after its introduction, Cyril Pemberton wrote a paper for the *Hawaiian Planters Record*. Its general tone was almost one of celebration—relief that the toad had settled down, was breeding, and seemed content. Its food requirements were also easily satisfied.

Pemberton doesn't mention the toad's prowess in destroying beetles because populations needed time to build up and it was still too early to tell. But he never seems to doubt the toad's ability. He

All other methods of control of this pest have so far failed, and we strongly advocate the effective use, under favourable conditions, of this amphibian immigrant (*Bufo marinus*) which is doing its full share of benefit to our sugar industry and to which this International Congress should pay a tribute of gratitude.

—RAQUEL R. DEXTER, "The Food Habits of the Imported Toad, *Bufo marinus*, in the Sugar Cane Sections of Porto Rico," International Society of Sugar Cane Technologists, Fourth Congress, San Juan, Puerto Rico, March 1932, Bulletin no. 74, pp. 4–5

looks on the bright side and is so impressed with the attributes the toad may have that he writes with poetic feeling about the toads' melodic voice.

Cyril and his wife, Mildred even had their annual Christmas card specially designed. Their friends received season's greetings replete with a weather vane encompassing the four points of direction and perched atop was a dancing toad.

Toad fame was growing. To frustrated entomologists and desperate cane growers like the Queenslanders, *Bufo* must have begun to seem irresistible.

At about this time, other, unseen forces were at work. There was a shake-up in personnel at the Bureau of Sugar Experiment Stations and Edmund Jarvis was moved from the Meringa Sugar Experiment Station (the Grub Station) at Gordonvale to Brisbane headquarters. Then, to fill the vacancy, headquarters decided to retrieve Reg Mungomery from his current post at Bundaberg, where he had married and bought a home.[3]

In 1925, when he was in his early twenties and just starting out, Reg had been the entomologist at the Meringa Station with Jim Buzacott. Now, once

[3] J. H. Buzacott, M.B.E., "Notes on the Giant Toad," *Mulgrave Shire Historical Society*, Bulletin no. 64, February 1984.

 10

again, it was the original team, Mungomery and Buzacott back at Meringa, at the Grub Station, with the same old problem and no headway made for a decade.

In 1935, everything came together. All the pieces jelled nicely:

1. The sugarcane pest persisted.
2. The frustration of the cane farmers continued.
3. The toad had achieved fame.
4. Having been moved from Meringa to Bundaberg and back again to Meringa, Reg Mungomery was due some consideration from the Bureau.
5. The toad needed an Australian sponsor.*

Reg Mungomery got the job. As fellow worker Graham Hughes remembers, it would have been logical for Reg to grasp the opportunity—at last a big chance to do something for the cane grower. It would have been natural for Reg to be eager to

---

* These events as viewed after more than half a century by Graham Hughes, who had just finished University and had entered the workforce in his first job at the Meringa Station.

take up the idea of bringing in this toad to see what it would do here.

At last some hope. The Bureau of Sugar Experiment Stations couldn't hesitate any longer. The situation was desperate: the cane growers never let up on their demand—"*Do* something!" The despair of the times, with the beetles in flight, had become well-nigh intolerable.

Now that they had what appeared to be a report that this animal was doing a wonderful job elsewhere, it looked as though they could expect a similar job here. They'd tried everything else and the time for more action had come. In those days decision-making was not the formal structured procedure it is today. It was then a matter of simply steeling themselves to be game and declaring, "Let's have a go for it!" They approached the Commonwealth authorities for permission to import the toad. The Bureau had to show that the toad would consume only night-flying insects, and as the pests in the sugarcane fields were all night fliers, permission was granted.

Now that the time for action had come, it centred on Reg Mungomery. Reg was a steadfast man, one who could look you straight in the eye. He was clean-cut, fresh-faced, square-jawed, and

REG MUNGOMERY,
MERINGA STATION
GRUB FIGHTER

forthright. He'd left Bundaberg behind and was back at Meringa with the grub problem and he possessed the dedication to try to solve it.

In April 1935, Reg Mungomery was granted an overseas trip to Hawaii for his appointed task. In future years, he would write many papers on *Bufo marinus* for the *Cane Growers' Quarterly Bulletin*, but in his first he called it by another name. No longer was it the "Introduced Tropical American Toad"; now it was the "Giant American Toad."

In a paper in the *Proceedings of the International Society of Sugar Cane Technologists*, Reg reports that on the night of 1 June, 1935, with the aid of the headlights of a motorcar, he and Pemberton captured 102 toads on various lawns in the suburbs of Honolulu. Equal numbers of males and females were selected in an age range from half- to full-grown. This was so the toads could mature at different periods and stagger the egg-laying seasons.[4] The object was to get the toads to breed in their new home, and everything was done to ensure that this would happen.

The 102 toads were packed in two cases among

> The latest importation of the Giant American Toad into Queensland will mark another step in the gradual conquest of the warmer regions of the earth by this remarkable animal.
>
> —R. W. MUNGOMERY, "The Giant American Toad (*Bufo marinus*)," *Cane Growers' Quarterly Bulletin*, 1 July 1935, p. 22

---

[4] R. W. Mungomery, "A Short Note on the Breeding of *Bufo marinus* in Captivity," *Proceedings of the International Society of Sugar Cane Technologists*, 1935, p. 589.

some dampened wood shavings and during the nineteen-day ocean voyage they were moistened from time to time with a little water. When they arrived in Gordonvale, only one had died. The remaining 101 were somewhat thin and dehydrated but swelled out as soon as they were placed in water and quickly resumed their normal bloated appearance.[5] These were the progenitors of the entire toad population now resident in Australia.

They were bedded down in a pond specially built for them by Jim Buzacott while Reg had been in Hawaii. The pond was designed to entertain them and prevent escape but it still offered the captives every creature comfort. It was built of concrete, twelve feet across, deeper in the centre, with a revolving sprinkler to aerate and replenish the water. Hyacinths, water lilies, and other aquatic plants were placed in the pond and along the edges; taro, ferns, and the like were planted among the rocks to simulate natural conditions so the toad could have shelter in daylight and would feel at

[5] Ibid., pp. 589–90.

home. The pond and its surrounds were enclosed in an octagonal framework structure covered with chicken-wire netting.[6]

It was then midwinter in Queensland—the cold and dry months regarded as an unsuitable time of year for toads—so every care was taken to ensure their welfare. The toads were to be kept in their

The evening song of the male toad can now be readily heard on quiet evenings in taro patches, rice fields and reservoirs where the species is well established. The song can perhaps be best described as a rapid succession of deep flute-like notes. By some, it has been described as resembling the sound of a distant diesel engine; others have compared it with the muffled sound of a motorcycle in the distance. The females are not considered as finished and ardent vocalists as the males.

—PEMBERTON, op. cit., p. 192

---

[6] Buzacott, op. cit.

captive quarters until the start of the wet season in November or December, and if no egg-laying had taken place by then, they were to be set free in an appropriate locality.

Imagine, then, the elation when their efforts were rewarded only six days after the captives had been installed. On the morning of 1 July, long strips of a gelatinous substance enclosing jet-black eggs were found entangled among the water weeds. Three days later the eggs hatched. The tadpoles were plentiful and, to supplement the algae from the hyacinths, were fed a nourishing diet based on Cyril Pemberton's prescription of boiled rice, cooked Cream of Wheat, and Carnation flakes.[7] For Reg Mungomery it was a personal triumph, as this was the first time the toad had been successfully bred in captivity. Henceforth—and ever after—Reg would feel a sense of responsibility toward his protégé and would champion the cause of *Bufo marinus* in Queensland.

My dad was an Irishman and he was very, very pleased about the whole affair and more. So he said this and I quote, "We've got these bloody grubs by the balls this time, and we'll go on to bigger and brighter things."
—TIP BYRNE

[7] Pemberton, op. cit., p. 188, and Mungomery, "A Short Note on the Breeding of *Bufo marinus* in Captivity," p. 590.

C·A·N·E TOADS

Sitting Pretty

TWO

New war to be waged against greyback cane grubs by giant American toad: The first consignment of 102 toads has arrived from Honolulu this week and will be taken to Meringa for breeding purposes and later distributed throughout affected areas. The toads have done splendid work in keeping down insect pests in Barbados, the West Indies and Hawaii.

—*CAIRNS POST*,
22 June 1935

So far, so good. The toads were here. They were publicly welcomed in *The Queenslander* of 27 June 1935, which prophesied that the toads would "prove a very useful addition to the fame of North Queensland."

Almost immediately upon their arrival, the toads had set the minds of their sponsors at rest by breeding profusely for the first time ever in the captive state. Eggs, tadpoles, toadlets were in abundance. All that remained was dispersal to the fields for the eradication of the beetle and its grub.

Reg Mungomery's scrapbook offers details of

19

They'd put the young toadlets in kerosene tins and put them on the train, a rail motor actually. It stopped at the Boogan railway station where I'd pick them up. Or I went into Innisfail railway station and picked up toads and carried them into South Johnstone and released them into pools and creeks.

One day I was advised by telephone that a consignment was coming in. It was the height of the season—my busiest time of year when I was flat out destroying cane grubs. Well, I picked them up

the first liberations, starting on 18 August 1935. Toadlets in batches of one hundred to five hundred were sent to specific sites of the Mulgrave and Hambledon districts—colourful places with names like Boggy Creek, Bull Paddock, O'Leary's Creek, Moree Swamps, and Sawmill Pocket.

Tadpoles in beer bottles and toadlets in tins were delivered to the various sites. Requests for toadlets from other northern districts began to come through directly to the Meringa Station or through Brisbane headquarters. For a while, dispersals and liberations were made and orders faithfully filled—more or less.

Back in 1935, George Wilson, on the staff of a local Cane Pest Destruction Board, had the responsibility of being chief toad distributor. As such, he was in a spot of bother because it was awkward to keep an accurate tally. Toadlets and tadpoles would slither through his grasp, and if he was supposed to deliver five hundred to a specific site, his desire to be efficient was confounded by the number sliding away. But, he contends, it really didn't matter, because the toads seemed to be more than plentiful. Deliveries had been made to grateful recipients

20

in dispersal areas, but all through Queensland there were still cane farmers waiting anxiously for liberations; they were counting on the toad.

Now another element comes in and that is people—ordinary people—who were not part of the Bureau of Sugar Experiment Stations and people not at all concerned with growing sugar. Even this early, just when it all seemed so promising, a trickle of objections began coming through. Dogs that foamed at the mouth after contact with the toad? Just wash out their mouths and they'll be fine. Bees that disappeared down toad gullets? Just raise the hives off the ground and you'd be right. Fowls that got sick from toad-contaminated water? Nonsense! Superstition! That's what it was! It's apparent that complaints were usually scoffed at, treated lightly, and laughed away.

But not everyone was inclined to be lighthearted, especially one Walter W. Froggatt, then president of the New South Wales Naturalist Society, who was the first to try to raise his voice publicly against *Bufo*. This prompted Cyril Pemberton, who was visiting in Sydney from Hawaii, to write to Reg in Queensland. He informed Reg that he'd seen Froggatt in Sydney and learned about

but I couldn't take time straight off to distribute them. So I had to take them home with me—put them in the bathtub and filled it with water. They kept trying to hop out and would've made it too, but I kept the wife there and whenever a toad came up the side of the tub, she'd push him back in again.
—GEORGE WILSON,
South Johnstone Cane Pest
Destruction Board, 1935

We had enough toads by the end of the first year to establish the whole thing for all of Queensland. There were toads in the cane fields, toads around the city street lights—sometimes about eighty-strong in circles all around—and toads in the rubbish tips. When they were disturbed there, the noise was like a crackling. It was like a grass fire sweeping through. Anyway, there were so many of them, I could stop the distributing part of my job and go back to the pest control office in South Johnstone.

—GEORGE WILSON

his paper prepared for the *Sydney Morning Herald*. Pemberton wrote that the editor had returned it to Froggatt, refusing to publish it because he thought it was "greatly alarming" and that, as the government had allowed its entry, there must be some value in the toad.

Reg was quick to appreciate Pemberton's point of view. In Reg's own piece, "A Survey of the Feeding Habits of the Giant Toad (*Bufo marinus* L.) and Notes on Its Progress Since Its Introduction into Queensland," which he wrote for the Sugar Cane Technologists' conference in Mackay in 1936, he stated that it seemed almost inevitable that all attempts to progress would meet with totally unwarranted opposition.

Nevertheless, suspicions were being heard and they rebounded. The Federal Health Department, then under the ministry of the illustrious Joe Lyons, had been established with quarantine as its primary concern. Its Director General of Quarantine Matters was Dr. John Howard Lidgett Cumpston, who had held the job since March 1921 and was hardly short of experience. In early December 1935 this Federal Health Department seemed to have second thoughts. A ban was imposed on the toad. It specified that liberations were to continue only in

those areas where toads had already been distributed—Cairns, Gordonvale, Innisfail, and Tully—and they were not to venture farther afield into new areas. Impatient cane growers outside the specified areas would have to bide their time.

Meanwhile Mr. Froggatt had recovered from the rebuff of the *Sydney Morning Herald* and, undeterred, had his article accepted by the *Australian Naturalist* magazine.

Sighs of exasperation must have been forthcoming from Reg but, fortified by Pemberton's philosophy of the inevitability of all progress having opposition, he was able to rise above the attack and retaliate. He made his stand with a scathing piece, "In Defense of *Bufo marinus*," that held Froggatt up to ridicule. He describes Froggatt's views as pathetic and claims that he misquotes, that his article is full of inaccuracies, and that his criticisms are worthless. He questions Froggatt's motives and seems to rap him smartly over the knuckles, scolding all the while.

Now, with Froggatt dismissed as a crank, Reg could devote himself fully to the task at hand, that of reversing the government ban. There were growers in the North who wanted a liberation of toads and who had been patiently waiting and he was

It is inevitable that all progress has opposition.

—CYRIL PEMBERTON to Reg Mungomery, 14 October 1935

Just fancy that coming from the Commonwealth authorities! When as you say the toads are well entrenched here, and they must ultimately reach saturation point. Their ruling would be the subject of loud laughter, were it not for the fact that we have such a crowd of imbeciles at the head of affairs in those departments, which unfortunately, have the power to veto our work.

—REG MUNGOMERY to Cyril Pemberton, 7 January 1936

In these notes I am calling the attention of all nature lovers to the danger, which, to me, threatens the ground fauna of Australia, through the action of the Queensland Government in introducing this large toad, to liberate in the sugar cane plantations to feed upon the beetles that destroy the sugar cane roots. . . . Up to the present these big omnivorous toads have been liberated only on island

anxious to satisfy them. He undertook a detailed scientific examination, performing autopsies on toads to ascertain what they were eating, and sent the compiled statistics to the federal authorities. With this step he was able to convince the Health Department that the toad was innocent of crime: it was not eating any insect that could be considered beneficial in any way. The ban was lifted in October 1936 and the plan came to full fruition.

Toad liberations and dispersals were now possible to all the sugar areas in Queensland. Away they went. Toads to Babindi, Ingham, and Bambaroo. Toads to Giru, Ayr and Mackay. And toads to Bundaberg and Isis—all the cane-growing districts that had so eagerly waited out the year in anticipation.[1]

The great experiment was in full fling, and its progress can be charted through the pages of the *Annual Reports* of the Bureau of Sugar Experiment Stations.

The 1935 entry noted the optimistic introduction of the Giant American Toad, but the covering note was cautious and hedged its bets by saying

---

[1] R. W. Mungomery, "The Present Situation Regarding the Giant American Toad in Queensland," *Cane Growers' Quarterly Bulletin*, 1 July 1937, p. 12.

areas, but the possibilities of the spread of these creatures over an immense area like Australia with all kinds of climate is something different. . . . Nature has provided toads with small glands on the sides of the body which secrete an acrid fluid, and this can be discharged when seized or frightened. If seized by any dog or cat, they will be dropped at once and given a wide berth next time they are met with. . . . They are insectivorous, but nothing comes amiss to them. All our small ground fauna will become their prey, and all our curios, mostly harmless, and often useful ground insects in forest and field will vanish. The eggs and nestlings of all our ground nesting birds will be snapped up by these night-hunting marauders. All our frogs

that should the toad fall short of the hopes of eliminating the sugar pests, there is little doubt that the importation will be more than justified by the destruction of other pests.

The 1936 report presented statistics on the toad's breeding capacity. But later that same year Reg Mungomery was still defending his charge, claiming the Bureau's judgement had been sound. In the following year, 1937, the *Annual Report* noted the liberation and dispersal of toads to all areas formerly under restriction and stated that favourable reports had already been received on the toad's work in reducing insect pests in vegetable gardens and household pests such as cockroaches.

and lizards, most valu-
able insectivorous crea-
tures, will be in danger
of their lives. . . . There
is no limit to their
westward range, and
those originally natives
of tropical regions, will
probably adapt them-
selves to our mountain
ranges, and even reach
the river banks and
swamp lands in the in-
terior. . . . This great
toad, immune from ene-
mies, omnivorous in its
habits, and breeding all
the year round, may
become as great a pest
as the rabbit or the
cactus.
—WALTER W. FROGGATT,
Australian Naturalist,
January 1936

—Mrs. Barbara J. Stoddard,
secretary of the Linnean Society of New South Wales, whose
letter granted the use of Mr.
Froggatt's photo, also wrote,
"I hope your book will be a
great success. When it becomes a best-seller, perhaps
you may be interested to know
of our tax deductible Scientific
Research Fund which is always grateful for any dona-
tion."

"There, Prendergast, your cockroach worries are over."

It had now been three years—a long time to
wait for results—but Reg and his team were still
optimistic. The 1938 entry confirmed the presence
of toads in all Queensland sugar areas where white
grubs were causing noticeable injury.

The minutes of the Cane Pest Board Conference
held at the Meringa Station in 1938 reveal that Reg
Mungomery was again on the defensive, attacking
those newspapers that had publicized the unattrac-

tive traits of the toad. He claimed that such stories were reminiscent of ancient and mediaeval times when the toad was considered a deadly enemy. He was fearful that the toad's mission was being thwarted. He had heard that small boys were killing toads because they feared for their pets being poisoned and called for this slaughter to cease.

Reg suggested a plan that he thought could be helpful. He asked that the delegates to the conference see fit to pass a resolution that the toads be protected under government law—whether the Animals Protection Act of 1925 or the Fauna Protection Act of 1937.[2]

It must have been that the delegates to the conference did not see fit, as the proposal was not acted upon. Nevertheless, it was somehow beginning to dawn that the good intentions of the miracle cure were being misconstrued by an uninformed public—and that those same intentions were being sabotaged.

In 1939, four years after the toad's arrival, the Bureau of Sugar Experiment Stations still seemed optimistic, but in their summation that year in the *Annual Report* the toad had lost a bit of its shine.

[Froggatt's] protest is somewhat belated for already *Bufo marinus* is present in thousands in the North Queensland cane fields and moreover, *Bufo marinus* is now here to stay.

———
—REG MUNGOMERY, "In Defense of *Bufo marinus*"

This introduction into Queensland was made only after a careful analysis of the pros and cons, and, according to the behaviour of the toads up to the present, there appears to be no reason for the assumption that we have made an error in our judgement.

———
—R. W. MUNGOMERY, "A Survey of the Feeding Habits of the Giant Toad (*Bufo marinus* L.) and Notes on Its Progress Since Its Introduction into Queensland," *Proceedings of the Queensland Society of Sugar Cane Technologists*, 7th Annual Conference, Mackay, Queensland, 1936, p. 74

---

[2] R. W. Mungomery, "Toad Protection," *Minutes of the Cane Pest Board Conference*, Meringa, 1938, p. 36.

They noted that there could be some problems in the high and dry red volcanic soils. The toads, it seems, were not all that keen to stay in those fields for the job at hand unless "some special inducement is offered them to remain there."

The next year, 1940, was a bad year in the cane fields. It was a bad year for beetles because there were more of them. It was a bad year, too, for growers and for cane stalks. It was also a bad year for toads. But even worse was the Bureau of Sugar Experiment Stations' admission in the *Annual Report* that the toads were not devoting themselves to the specified job at hand.

All that wishful thinking hadn't worked.

The next year, 1941, saw the arrival in Gordonvale of Dr. Janos Brody, a newly appointed medical officer for the Mulgrave Shire. Dr. Brody supplied the shire's Historical Society with his first impressions of the area. Describing the cane paddocks filled with patches of yellow stunted cane, he told how the beetles could be swept up by the bucketful on the verandahs of the homes and how men still went into the paddocks with canisters of the evil-smelling carbon disulphide for fumigation.

Outwardly, it might have appeared that nothing much had changed, but actually, there had been one small, almost imperceptible change. Dr. Brody, in his piece for the Mulgrave Shire Historical Society, referred to the "cane toad." No longer was it the "Giant American Toad," "introduced" or "imported." It was as though it had been legally adopted, had its name changed, and seemed to belong to the land upon which it squatted.

The cane toad was first released in the Gordonvale area in an attempt to control the cane grub. Unfortunately, the toads preferred to sit under the street lights and enjoy a free meal of the insects attracted by the lights. . . . One old lady kept a cane toad as a pet, feeding it on soup bones and Vegemite* on Sao biscuits and [it] thrived on this diet. Eventually, it grew to the size of a small cat. The cane grubs thrived as well and were not controlled until BHC became available.

———————
—J. BRODY, "First Impressions of Gordonvale, 1941," *Mulgrave Shire Historical Society,* Bulletin no. 61, September 1983

———————
—Vegemite is a yeast spread. On toast or biscuits it's considered to be standard nutritional fare for growing children.

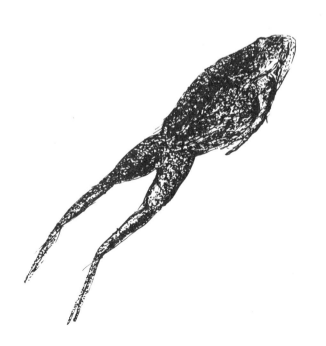

C·A·N·E TOADS

Habits and Lifestyles

THREE

Settled in the sugarcane areas and hopping all over the land, cane toads are under close scrutiny, but to truly know them, first we have to find them. They spend the daytime hiding from sunlight, which tends to dehydrate them. At dusk they emerge and, even under this soft light, a glance confirms that they are repulsive.

A cane toad can just about sit comfortably in the palm of an adult male hand. They are from four to six inches long and about four inches wide, the females being larger than the males. They are stocky, short and broad, khaki brown in colour

There's a lot of popular misconceptions about cane toads, one of which is that they feel disgusting to touch, but this isn't true at all. They feel quite dry, not slimy; their skin is slightly rough but it does have a nice silky feeling and you don't get warts from them.

—BETTINA DALTON,
ranger, Queensland National
Parks and Wildlife Service

Those Buffalo Merino toads could really smoke—they really loved them!

—PAT WHITE,
cane farmer, Gordonvale

with bumpy skin. The male has skin like sandpaper; the female's skin is smooth. Their underside, denied any light, is marbled brown on a pale colourless background. Their mouths have a dour downward pull on each side. Their eyes have heavy hoods and seem only half awake and stagnant. Just behind each hooded eye is a large gland full of toxins that contain a venom potentially deadly to animals and humans.

The venom gives the cane toad a built-in defence system. Any animal or reptile that views the toad as a possible meal partakes of a deadly poison pill and the attacker dies along with its victim. But putting this role into reverse, the toad is still in the position of advantage. Cyril Pemberton said it would eat anything that could pass down its throat. Everything and anything is edible and entirely agreeable to its palate, including its very own young. Even cigarette butts still alight that larrikins at the pubs used to toss to them. They'd go for bottle caps because they shine and glint and even Ping-Pong balls because they bounce.

 34

But for ordinary daily cane toad fare, it's speed that counts. The sleepy demeanour of the cane toad belies its quick movements when something attracts its attention. One minute there's a moveable object; the next second it is no more—vanished into the toad interior.

Cane toads eat all the insects at hand—that is, *ground*-dwelling insects. And now, of course, too late the idea dawns that the cane beetles which were meant to be its victims are not ground-dwelling insects. The beetles are in the air and mostly stay there, while the cane toad, which cannot fly, is on the ground and always stays there. If the cane beetles are in the fields when there is no cover on the ground, cane toads, avoiding sunlight, won't go into fields without cover. The natural aptitudes and lifestyle of the cane toad make it almost

Another misconception is that just by touching them, the cane toads will exude their poison, and this is also not true. For a toad like this to exude any of its poison from its glands it has to be severely harassed; for instance, being picked up in a dog's mouth and really severely shaken.

—BETTINA DALTON

A carpenter bee . . . was snapped up and passed down the insatiable *Bufo* gullet. This bee possesses an exceedingly powerful sting. . . . After swallowing such a fiery creature, *Bufo* was observed to execute a few abdominal motions suggestive of the Hawaiian "hula" dance. . . . Freshly decapitated centipedes, which are still able to crawl, are eaten apparently without fear of injury; but the many legs of the large centipedes are usually able to cling over the mouth or head of the toad so tightly that the process of swallowing such a long object is often accomplished only after much laborious gulpings and pushing and pawing with the front feet.

———
—C. E. PEMBERTON, "Local Investigations on the Introduced Tropical American Toad, *Bufo marinus*," *Hawaiian Planters Record*, vol. 38, no. 2 (1934), p. 190

completely useless for any confrontation with the beetles. So any expectations that cane toads could eliminate cane beetles belong in the realm of whimsical fantasy.

According to George Wilson and Dr. Brody, cane toads congregate around streetlights in the night-time and loll about like derelict drunks licking up whatever insects drop onto the ground—everything they can flick onto their sticky tongues.

Somehow this scene seems to fit. It's realistic. The days of the cane toad being cossetted were soon over. No more the royal treatment they'd had when they first arrived. Now they had to fend for themselves and it seemed that nobody was overly concerned or cared much what they did. But even though their mission was aborted and may have left their sponsors blushing, the cane toads, with nobody's blessing, still had the advantage: they felt the fair breath of freedom in this newer world. Wherever they could, they sheltered from the daytime sun and, seemingly left to their own devices to do what they pleased, it pleased them to breed and that's what they did.

At the peak of midsummer breeding, the males precede the females to freshwater breeding sites—

They weren't much use at all as far as the cane beetles were concerned, but they did manage to get rid of a lot of stray dogs. The dogs would be attracted to these moving toads and grab 'em and, of course, the Buffalo Merino's only protection was his poison sac. He used to let the dogs have it and quite a few dogs died.
—PAT WHITE

The male cane toad has sticky patches on the nuptial pads inside his thumbs which he uses to stick firmly to the female and prevents any other randy male from knocking him off.

A normal female cane toad can lay as many as 20,000 eggs in an egg string mass and she can do this three times a year. That's 60,000 eggs that could become 60,000 tadpoles—60,000 toadlets—60,000 cane toads.

Animal ecologist Dr. Robert Floyd describes their passion as insatiable. He has observed

any water that is not fast-flowing—billabongs, transient pools, ditches, or creeks. These inspired males sound a mating call (those flute-like sounds described so lyrically by Cyril Pemberton in Hawaii) to lure the female. A particular pitch wins her. The male clasps her. The clasping is called "amplexus," the male mounting the female's back and pressing his nuptial pads into her armpits. Amplexus can last for many hours, until eventually she pilots him into the water for spawning. A long translucent string with black eggs about a millimetre wide (about the size of a pinhead) dotted along it is exuded behind them as she surges forward, sporadically shedding eggs that are externally fertilized as he releases sperm. In three days, the eggs hatch into tadpoles.[1]

The mating procedure was originally observed and annotated in the early days of the Meringa Station pond. It is because Australia's cane toads had originally been bred in captivity that Reg Mungomery had the advantage of being able to study them. It was Reg who discovered an idiosyncrasy in them not known before—that is, that cane toads can change their sex.[2]

Reg selected the original clutch of 102 toads in equal numbers of male and female, the male being slightly smaller and not as smooth to the touch as the female. Making allowance for the one that had died en route, the batch was mustered at intervals, and early in 1936 a count was made of those in the pond. It was then found that the tally of females had increased while the

cane toads, especially after a rain, in a frenzy of breeding. Several hundred males wait for females and fight each other for the one of their choice. Dr. Floyd says that females have been seen carrying four males on their backs, each one trying to achieve amplexus.

When in full chorus, calling males will attempt to clasp in amplexus any object about the dimensions of a toad, including the footwear of intruding naturalists.
—I. R. STRAUGHAN, formerly with the University College of Townsville Zoology Department

---

[1] I. R. Straughan, "The Natural History of the 'Cane Toad' in Queensland," *Australian Natural History*, September 1966, p. 231.

---

[2] R. W. Mungomery, "Sex Reversal in the Giant Toad," *Cane Growers' Quarterly Bulletin*, 1 July 1936, p. 7.

Cane toad passion casts its glow upon a diverse range of subjects, including feet, hands, and even hunks of mud.

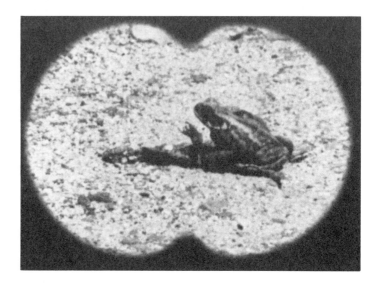

On December 27, 1959, on a dirt road three miles east of Bingal Bay, an adult male toad was observed during amplexus with an adult female toad. At least three factors appeared quite unique about this situation. First, the female was dead and had been for some time. It appeared as if she had fallen victim to a car. The limbs were already stiff, abdomen greatly distended and the smell of putrefaction about her. Next, it appears strange that the male should be so intent as to fail to notice the female's condition. And last, the time and place we encountered this pair was unusual. It males had decreased and that somehow three males had managed to become females.

Evidently, mysterious workings of the interior juices seem to transform some closet males into egg-producing females. What matters is that second-hand, re-created females do not produce as many eggs as a cane toad that is female from the start. But celebrations are still in order: in this case, the less, the better, and no need to lament.

After the initial importees had been established in the Meringa Station pond in June 1935, it was estimated that by March 1937 no fewer than

was at 1400 hours on a sunny afternoon—in the middle of the road (and no water in sight for the depositing of eggs if that could have been even remotely possible). The sexual drive appears strong enough in these toads to explain his accepting her but his continuance through a possible eight hours of daylight does seem rather strange.

—DANIEL WILHOFT,
American Fulbright Scholar,
"An Unusual Act of Amplexus
in *Bufo marinus*"

1,560,000 eggs had been laid and that about 62,000 toadlets had been caught and distributed.[3]

Eggs in the millions require breeding sites—but the cane toad is not choosy and demonstrates remarkable adaptability. It's been said that any billabong, water hole, transient pool, ditch, or sluggish backwater creek will do. Actually, all they seem to require is enough wetness. Scientists have related how at Amos Bay, south of Cooktown, tyre

---

[3] J.H.B., "How Frequently Do Giant Toads Produce Eggs?," *Cane Growers' Quarterly Bulletin*, 1 July 1936, p. 25.

tracks had left indentations on a tidal flat and water from heavy rains had accumulated in them. The cane toads used these leftover puddles of hot, shallow, and slightly brackish water and had successfully bred in them in great numbers.[4]

Cane toad ardour runs at fever pitch. At the Meringa Station, Reg noted that a mating pair of cane toads was caged without food for periods up to a month. At the end of this time, they were marked and released in the pond with access to the

[4] J. Covacevich and M. Archer, "The Distribution of the Cane Toad, *Bufo marinus*, in Australia and Its Effects on Indigenous Vertebrates," *Memoirs of the Queensland Museum*, 1975, p. 307.

normal food supply. Did they rush for the food as was expected? They did not. The male just went on clasping the female, his embrace not in the least relinquished because of his fasting ordeal.[5]

The cane toads gave a demonstration of their skill in an exhibit for the sugar industry at the Royal Agricultural Show in Brisbane soon after they arrived. The toads were displayed in an aquarium with hyacinths. The general public's desire for entertainment was fulfilled with a tremendous dis-

---

[5] R. W. Mungomery, "The Present Situation Regarding the Giant American Toad in Queensland," *Cane Growers' Quarterly Bulletin*, 1 July 1937, p. 67.

PAUL De Vine and a bucketful of cane toads he killed during one night.

Sexy toads give fish a caning

By COLIN CAMPBELL

SEX-crazed toads could have strangled at least 22 large goldfish belonging to the president of the Townsville aquarium society Paul De Vine.

Mr De Vine, of Railway Estate, does not believe the canetoad is dying out in North Queensland — he reckons they are all over his place.

He says he has killed "bucketfuls" — almost 200 — during the past few nights in an attempt to save his goldfish, which live in open ponds in his backyard.

According to Mr De Vine, the toads could be attempting to mount the goldfish, mistaking them for female toads, and covering their gills with their front paws, strangling or suffocating the fish.

"They breed in the vacant areas across the road and over in the national park areas.

"I've been out in the back yard every night in the last week with my net," he said.

He said that it was always the larger fish that were killed, probably because of the "breeding zeal".

On Thursday night he caught 70 toads and the next night he caught 40.

He says the dry weather is attracting the toads to his ponds.

James Cook University Zoologist Dr Ross Alford, who is involved in a major study of the canetoad, says that the strangling theory is possible as male canetoads have been known to drown females while trying to mate.

"Three or four males will hold the female under water until she drowns," he said.

Although there is a perceptible drop in the number of toads around Townsville, Dr Alford says there are large concentrations around ponds and freshwater areas at the moment.

"The mating season is unusually long — from around August to March — and males tend to stay around fresh water," he said.

He said there were plenty of toads to be found along Ross River and the various weirs.

"They are certainly not being wiped out in the North," he said.

play of fornication. The children were amazed; the mothers alarmed, and charged to supply answers to a frenzy of questions, were lost for words.

It is clear that it is in this area of amplexus—fornication, copulation, fucking, or whatever you choose to call it—that the cane toads' talents

45

lie. They're not selective. Of course, normal sexual partners are readily available and so much passionate amplexing goes on and on that it results in a population explosion—more and more cane toads where they're least expected.

Imagine having to mow a lawn with one cane toad to every two square metres (about 21.5 square feet). That so simple a task as mowing a suburban lawn once or perhaps twice a week could become an exercise in cane toad slaughter with all the trimmings of carcasses, guts, and stench is not a figment of an overstimulated imagination. That's how it *is*.

While the cane toads' amorous proclivities get it into mischief and bring it the wrong kind of attention, the toads haven't been prevented from continuing to do what they do best. Copious breeding and a more than plentiful abundance of eggs eventually got the toad into more diversified areas of Queensland. After all, not having a penchant for beetles, there was no reason for it to remain around the sugarcane fields, and so it moved on. It hopped along, exploring other areas, such as dry beef cattle country, forests of all kinds, sandy coastal plains, farmlands and pastures, and eventually suburban and urban areas.

The cane toad, by nature, is not choosy about *anything*. Food there is aplenty, with insects everywhere. Water is bound to be found—even brackish or rainwater puddles will do. And daytime shelter can be almost anything at all—shallow depressions under logs, drainpipes, debris, under cement slabs, rocks, and sheets of roofing iron, in potted plants in gardens, under fallen banana fronds, under crates and junk beneath houses.

The cane toad is a homebody and a creature of habit. Once it has established a spot as daytime shelter, it forms an attachment and keeps on returning to it. Be it ever so humble, there's no place

Only someone who has visited those parts of Queensland or New Guinea where the toad is most abundant can have any real concept of just how numerous the toads can become. Imagine walking on a garden lawn at night and having one toad to every two square metres. Thus, with every step that you take, toads are roving in front and on each side of you: a slowly moving sea of dark, shuffling, hopping creatures falling as they attempt to escape and jostling one another.

—M. J. TYLER, *Frogs* (London: Collins, 1976), p. 80.

MAKE A HOME FOR YOUR GARDEN'S GUARDIANS

FOR A GARDEN FREE of insect pests, I advise encouraging toads to make their homes somewhere among your vegetables and flowers. Because we have found them effective in controlling bugs that would feed on the leaves and stems of our delphiniums, we place little clay homes for our toads right in the plant rows. We take an 8-inch clay pot, chip out a small portion as shown, and set it up in an inverted position in a cool, shady spot.

like home, comfortable and familiar. The toad also has a sort of loyalty about breeding, but that loyalty is not faithfulness to another toad. It's for a place—

the water hole to which it returns time after time for breeding and spawning.

The new issue of juveniles, having metamorphosed from eggs to tadpoles to toadlets, are the ones that force the spread of the population. They have to exert every caution in regard to finding their own shelter spots because they could be cannibalized by the adult cane toads already in residence. As winter draws on, conditions become drier and accommodation harder to find.

Hence, the younger generation has to strike out for itself and it moves on. Moving on, cane toads expand the margins of their occupied area and begin breeding for themselves in new water holes, producing more toads and creating an ever-expanding continuity.

From having been established and distributed by man in 1936 to all the sugar areas along the Queensland coast, the cane toad, at last count by 1981, had spread under its own volition to occupy an area that covers 785,000 kilometres (470,000 miles), almost half of Queensland, and is also established in the area surrounding Byron Bay in

Cane toads are something that have been considered in Australian society as uniquely Queensland. When we were starting up a satirical magazine we wanted something that was Queensland and yet was spreading to other States like a menace.

—ANNE JONES, editor, Cane Toad Times

the north of New South Wales. Its distribution extends from the Archer River on the Cape York Peninsula to the Tweed River on the Queensland–New South Wales border. The overall average rate of increase in the total area occupied has been 8.1 percent a year and it advances at a rate of 27 kilometres (16 miles) a year.

It's heading toward the Northern Territory and Kakadu and nobody there wants it.

C·A·N·E TOADS

Uses and Functions

The proposal to commemorate the cane toad was brought before the Bicentennial Committee of the Mulgrave Shire Council in 1986 to record a unique part of Australia's history and the sugar industry. The original idea came from the Gordonvale Historical Society. It was for a statue to be erected at Gordonvale where the toad was first introduced—just off the road near the Meringa Experiment Station. The statue was to represent a cane toad squatting on a pedestal with a plaque—altogether about two metres high. It was meant to be something like the dog on the tucker box five miles from Gundagai. The type of thing I thought would get around by word of mouth and people would flock here just to say they'd seen it.

—MAX ACKLAND,
Mulgrave Shire councillor

FOUR

The Northern Territory doesn't want the cane toads. Be that as it may, it's nevertheless different in Queensland, where the toads have been ensconced for more than fifty years. Queenslanders have had plenty of time to become conditioned and some have developed degrees of benign tolerance. A kind of folklore has grown up about them—a cane toad subculture. For example, in Patrick Cook's cartoons, a former Queensland Premier was always drawn with cane toads on or around him.

Some Queenslanders would have liked the cane toad to receive official recognition. Councillor Max Ackland wanted to commemorate the cane toad by erecting a statue to it in Gordonvale.*

---

* *Surely, this bastard can't be in his right frame of mind. Fancy anyone wanting to erect a monument or a stone or some form of remembrance to this creature that's been brought in.—Tip Byrne*

Such a pity that it didn't come to fruition —and I might add— without spending a penny of ratepayers' money because it was a Bicentennial project. I felt that we missed the boat a little. The kids could've sat on the cane toad's shoulders and what not. And anyone having their picture taken alongside it would've looked beautiful by comparison. It's been changed—can you imagine it—to a drink fountain—or something. I told the councillors they were narrow-minded. I told them that—in a nice way, of course. No imagination! Absolutely none! No imagination at all!
—MAX ACKLAND

It's difficult to go anywhere in Queensland without coming across references to, or idolatry concerned with, the cane toad, because they are ubiquitous. They're absolutely everywhere. People are brought up with them and the Queenslanders are terribly protective of them it would seem, although something as obnoxious as the cane toad you would expect would have been eradicated by now. Far from it. Because Queensland's got them and nobody else has got them, I think they regard them with a sort of perverted reverence.

—PATRICK COOK, cartoonist

Max went to a taxidermist to help him decide on the squatting position and he obtained little stuffed toads to show how it would look. He had an estimate that the statue would cost $3,500 and he compiled an official dossier. When the proposal got to Council level, he conveyed all this information with great enthusiasm and was stunned to find that he couldn't sway all the other councillors. The idea was rejected, and Max's disappointment was keenly felt.

The notion may have been quashed originally, but since then new attitudes have surfaced. On November 21, 1988, *Cairns Post* reporter Bernard Lane stated that the issue of a cane toad monument had reinsinuated itself.

Bill Prien, a Chamber senior vice president, says he would like to see a statue in a prominent position. And Jim Buzacott, Jr., whose father worked with Reg Mungomery at the Meringa Station outside Gordonvale, is not upset by talk of toad statues. He suggested to his sister that the Mulgrave Shire

Any North Queensland town could erect a Big Cane Stalk, but only Gordonvale could create the Big Toad. We've got more connections with the cane toad than anywhere else in Australia because it was released here. I'm all for anything that promotes Gordonvale.

—WARREN PITT,
Gordonvale Chamber of
Commerce

MULGRAVE SHIRE COUNCIL, 1987–88.
COUNCILLOR MAX ACKLAND TOP LEFT.

Council should erect a giant cane toad near Gordonvale or Meringa.

So it could even yet come to pass that the original idea will blossom in artistic form in the sculptured shape of *Bufo marinus*.

But aside from public homage and formal honour, there are still plenty of Queenslanders who steadfastly contend that the cane toad warrants their affection. This is substantiated by what animal ecologist Dr. Robert Floyd describes as their homophilic characteristic—that is, cane toads love humans. Because humans meet their needs by providing food and shelter, water for breeding space, and lights that attract insects, cane toads thrive close to humans.

Some humans, like Elvie Greig, treat cane toads almost like pets. Elvie believes that toads are smart. She'll tell you about how they get to know you—that they know where to hide and where to find food. She says they have a sense of smell, for if there's food put out, she's seen them head for it in a straight line in the proper direction. She believes you could tame this small creature and train it to do just about anything.

Bettina Dalton, the ranger with the Queensland

 56

Early in '47 we had moved to the coast. One morning, when our youngest, not quite two years old, was on his way back from the WC down the backyard, we heard a fearful scream. I raced out to find him confronted by a thing the size of a football and, to my mind, oozing venom and viciousness. . . . A quick grab and I had the laddie safe, if shaken, in the house. The trusty rifle was the only means of attack, but after absorbing many rounds, the thing still squatted, damaged but unmoved. Next best thing was to grab a sheet of corrugated iron for a shield and the wood axe. With many a quick dart and a lunge, I was able to reduce it to mince meat.

A year or so after the big kill, a neighbour remarked with a grin that he'd seen me "do that big one over in the backyard." The whole street had been

watching secretly. Knowing that we were scared of toads, word had gone out to find a really big one to see how I'd react, because generally I was the first to be seen going to the WC of a morning. Their plan had been to rush in with a wheelbarrow, casually load up the inoffensive old lady toad, introduce everybody, and generally become good friends forever after. It had never occurred to them that I'd play Superman and rescue the family from a toad attack.

—MAURIE TRAYNOR,
Palmwood resident

ELVIE GRIEG

I'm not sure I'd call them pets exactly, but they're mates, as far as I'm concerned. They're just friends, friends, I s'pose because they're around the place. You get used to them and look for them.

The way they dart at things, the way they hide, the way they're cunning enough to peek out from behind things. They can be behind a leaf or something like that and if you're quick enough, you'll see their eyes watching wherever you go. And their singing—it's a friendly noise and I love it.

I started feeding toads Whiskettes [a brand of dried cat food] because they were robbing the cat's dish. So I put dishes of Whiskettes outside and they didn't come in then and everybody was happy. But after a while, they came in anyway and I really didn't mind.

I used to sit beside the stove and type. They started coming and would sit on my feet while I typed and I s'pose they were attracted by the tick-tick-ticking. It didn't occur to me to be frightened of them. The toads used to climb over each other to get the best position on my bare feet. So long as they could be in touch with my feet, they'd snuggle together and obviously snooze. It was really funny.

If anyone tried to hurt one of my toads—there'd be an awful lot of noise and they'd soon realize I wasn't a lady.

—ELVIE GREIG,
Redcliffe resident

National Parks and Wildlife Service, says cane toads are not distressed when they're picked up. In fact, she thinks they like it.

For three-year-old Monica, a toad is just as good as a toy. Monica is little and her toad is almost as big as she is, but it's her pet. The two of them frolic about together on the grass lawn.

Other old-timers besides Elvie Greig and Dave Sondergard, as well as little girls, seem to have fun and games with cane toads.

It would seem that the cane toad has had the effect of providing a form of amusement in its own way, but this is purely aesthetic. Surely, there must be a practical use for this creature imported for a specific task at which it failed. Queenslanders tried hard to fit it into other areas. A Queensland gardening journal of the 1960s describes the cane toad almost lovingly—squat, wistful-eyed—and sets it up as an insect destroyer supreme and the gardener's benefactor.

Hoppy hoppy rayta, getta felta tayta, a tissue, a tissue, we all fall down. He fell down. He done this. He fall down. Put him on the grass. Then I have a dream he's a lion.

When I tickle his tummy he really likes it. But if I tickle his feet he doesn't like it. She always jumps off me. She always keeps on jumping. She always plays games with me.

Sometimes I call him "Greeny" and sometimes I call him "Reddy" and sometimes I call him "Cane almost toad" and sometimes I call him "Dairy Queen."
—MONICA, three years old

59

It's quite a cocktail of toxic compounds, so I think people would do well to take care when handling toads. There are well-recorded instances of people dying as a result of eating toads in Fiji and in the Philippines. And so far as children are concerned, toads could be a real problem, particularly to babies or very young children who'd be attracted by the toad's hopping gait. If they were to squeeze the toad . . . if some of the bufotenine were to remain on their hands . . . if they were then to suck those hands and so forth—well, the results could be quite disastrous.

—DR. BOB ENDEAN

But it wasn't meant to be, because even in this humble task, the cane toad didn't find its niche. Another generation disputed its benefits in the garden and tossed it out. In January 1986, the *Courier Mail* ran a piece headlined "Toad Busters to the Rescue." It reported how two schoolgirls had embarked upon a profitable holiday venture. For a fee they would clear a yard of cane toads, demonstrating that a demand had arisen for this service.

Nicole, who has ambitions to become a veterinarian, doesn't mind the slaughter because "cane toads killed my little green tree frog and they kill butterflies and they poison my dog's water."

When we first came to Gordonvale, we had friends that had two little girls who kept cane toads as pets. Instead of little dollies, they had cane toads. They had little dresses made up for them, and beds and a doll's house. They dressed up these toads and tucked them into little beds. They carried them about, you know, wrapped up in baby bunting type of things like dollies. These girls had names for them. They set up tea parties. And they'd get these toads and scratch their tummies. And the things would lie back with their legs up in the air and just fall asleep. And they were the most contented, good little—and I suppose—*alive* little dollies that any girl could have. They would drag them around everywhere. The toads didn't mind at all.

—MARIE ROTH,
Gordonvale resident

So what's to be done with them?

STUFF THEM. John Kreuger, a Townsville taxidermist, has found a market for stuffed cane toads as souvenirs for tourists—or for local homebodies because they're good for laughs. His best-seller is just plain old *Bufo* in a natural squat on its own or elevated loftily onto a block of wood. His novelty range concentrates on larger cane toads standing upright on their hind legs, tizzed up to look formidable. A favourite that seems to have mass appeal is *Bufo* bearing a bottle of Bundaberg Rum.* Another stuffed toad carries a small cricket bat and has many fans among the "sports" from near and far.

Rumour has it that some erotica shops carry

---

* "Bundy" is an alcoholic beverage distilled by the Bundaberg Sugar Company in the northern Queensland town of the same name—the very town where Reg Mungomery had married and bought a home before he was transferred back to the Meringa Station at Gordonvale and voyaged to Hawaii to capture the toad and bring it back.

unusual stuffed cane toads amplexing (unnaturally for them) in the human missionary position.

DISSECT THEM. The cane toad has been used extensively as a laboratory animal for teaching and testing purposes. For many years it was the catalyst in pregnancy tests but has now been replaced. As a teaching aid in laboratories, the cane toad is at its best. It doesn't mind being handled, it doesn't care what it eats, and there are legions of them. The toad gradually filled in for frogs and then took over from them. Since the frog population declined mainly because of the predator toad, this appears to be a fair form of natural biological redemption.

COLLECT THEM. Collecting cane toads has become a cottage industry for innovative Queenslanders who sell them to laboratories or to people who stuff them or those who tan them. Some actually have made a commercial venture out of it and export toads to other countries. Peter Kraus earns his living by collecting cane toads. He sets forth from his home near Cairns on safaris to find enough toads to fill his orders. Peter supplies cane toads to secondary school and university laboratories for biological research.

Toad dissection is very nice. When you open up a toad, all the internal organs are very neat, nicely laid out and brightly coloured— lovely bright yellow fingery fat bodies and bits that are blue and bits that are red. It's all very clean and no smell. They are lovely dissection items.
—ROBERT FLOYD

BASH THEM. Many Queenslanders work out their frustrations on cane toads.

When I was an altar boy in the Sacred Heart Church in Theodore, Queensland, it automatically made me a member of the exclusive Dominic Savio Club in honour of the selfless boy-saint who used to trudge barefoot through the snow to serve mass every morning and twice on Sunday. At about the tender age of ten or eleven, because of what seemed to us to be a conspiracy between the Parish priest and our parents, all the altar boys were required to attend the Dominic Savio summer camp in tropical Prosperine. Apart from the long train journey, the homesickness, and the damp conditions, my only memory of this camp has to do with cane toads. Every night after we had washed the dishes and said our intercessary prayer to St. Dominic, we would vent our frustration by stealthily arming ourselves with torches and large sticks for a secret rebellion. In a scene reminiscent of *Lord of the Flies*, we would march out into the night and belt the cane toads to death. It established once and for all the loss of my innocence.

—GERRY CONNOLLY,
former altar boy

JUNE 1, 1967.

Dominic Savio Club, Theodore, Queensland.

BOYS' BEACON
ORGAN OF DOMINIC SAVIO CLUB

VOL. 12. No. 5.

Postal Address: Dominic Savio Club, Box 80, Oakleigh, S.E. 12, Vic.
Registered at the G.P.O., Melbourne for transmission by post as a periodical.

1c.

COOK THEM. The poisonous skin must be thoroughly removed. Then, *and only then,* toad legs can be treated much the same as frog's legs— a gourmet's delight.*

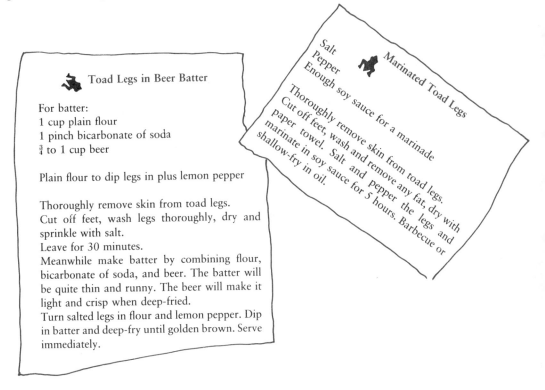

Toad Legs in Beer Batter

For batter:
1 cup plain flour
1 pinch bicarbonate of soda
$\frac{3}{4}$ to 1 cup beer

Plain flour to dip legs in plus lemon pepper

Thoroughly remove skin from toad legs.
Cut off feet, wash legs thoroughly, dry and sprinkle with salt.
Leave for 30 minutes.
Meanwhile make batter by combining flour, bicarbonate of soda, and beer. The batter will be quite thin and runny. The beer will make it light and crisp when deep-fried.
Turn salted legs in flour and lemon pepper. Dip in batter and deep-fry until golden brown. Serve immediately.

Marinated Toad Legs

Salt
Pepper
Enough soy sauce for a marinade

Thoroughly remove skin from toad legs.
Cut off feet, wash and remove any fat, dry with paper towel. Salt and pepper the legs and marinate in soy sauce for 5 hours. Barbecue or shallow-fry in oil.

* All recipes have been tested and tasted by a daring Queensland friend who requests that she remain anonymous.

Crumbed Toad Legs

Enough milk for legs to dip in
Enough plain flour for legs to roll in
Enough beaten egg for legs to dip in
Enough bread crumbs for legs to roll in

Thoroughly remove skin from toad legs.
Dip legs in milk, roll legs in plain flour, dip legs
in beaten egg, roll legs in bread crumbs. Deep-
fry legs in oil or shallow-fry in half butter and
half oil.

Toad Legs in White Wine

1 cup white wine
1 knob butter
1 finely chopped shallot
Parsley
1 teaspoon corn flour (cornstarch)
1 chicken stock cube
1 tablespoon thick cream
1 egg yolk

Thoroughly remove skin from toad legs. Cut
off feet and wash thoroughly. Salt and leave for
30 minutes.

Boil 1 cup white wine with knob of butter,
shallot, and parsley. Add salted toad legs and
cook until tender. Remove legs and keep warm.

Thicken wine sauce with corn flour (cornstarch).
Add stock cube and cream. Mix and cook for
1 minute. Remove from heat.

Add egg yolk and beat sauce with a fork. Return
toad legs to sauce. Serve hot, garnished with
lemon and parsley.

DR. GLEN INGRAM AND BETTE

Melissa Aprile with what may be the world's biggest toad.

GROW THEM. Some people take pleasure and pride in growing cane toads to be even more monstrous than they normally are. It's a simple process of feeding and weighing, and in this way cane toads give their owners a chance to indulge in a good-natured competitive camaraderie. Since cane toads have a naturally voracious appetite, they are keen to cooperate. Dr. Glen Ingram, senior curator, amphibia and birds, at the Queensland Museum, was the proud owner of Bette (because of her Bette Davis eyes), who is listed in the *Guinness Book of Records* as the heaviest toad in Australia and the third-largest toad in the world. At 1.806 kilograms (about four pounds), she was inferior in weight only to Jabba the Toad of Florida and Totally Awesome of Iowa. Other Australian toad hefties are Ross of Townsville, Mighty Martha of Bundaberg, and Dairy Queen of Gordonvale, the pet of little Monica, who likes to roll her over on her back and scratch her tummy. Dr. Ingram did the same for Bette, who always shut her eyes and played dead. Sadly, Bette doesn't play that game any more—or, in fact, any other game.*

This toad (unnamed), found by a Mackay resident, John Deambrogio, was thought to possibly be the world's largest—it weighed 1.8 kilograms (almost 4 pounds). Unfortunately, Mr. Deambrogio could not prove the claim—the toad died the day after this photograph was taken in December 1988.

Bulbous Bette has croaked, from old age

By GREG ROBERTS

BRISBANE: Bette, so-named because she had eyes like the actress Bette Davis, died of natural causes yesterday morning in her Gold Coast home.

On Sunday evening she had eaten a wholesome meal — a single one-day-old live chick — with no apparent ill-effects.

A post mortem examination will be conducted to establish why the biggest cane toad recorded in Australia croaked.

Bette officially became the world's third biggest toad last April when she tipped the scales at 1.806 kilograms. Soon after, however, she shot to the Number Two slot when the incumbent,

Totally Awesome of Iowa in the United States, passed away.

Now Jabba the Toad, of Florida, reigns supreme in the amphibian world, weighing in at a massive two kilograms.

Mr Geoff Smith, the animal care manager at Bette's last home, Koala Town on the Gold Coast, said the toad's demise "came as a surprise to everyone."

Bette was brought into the Queensland Museum in December 1987 by a Brisbane Aboriginal.

The curator of amphibians at the museum, Dr Glen Ingram, looked after the bulbous-eyed beast until handing her over to Koala Town two months ago.

Bette ... tipped the scales at 1.806 kilograms.

"I thought she was a lovely animal, despite the damage done by her fellows to the Queensland environment over the decades," Dr Ingram said. "It's sad that she's gone."

Bette will not be forgotten. A cast of her is to be made and put on display at the museum.

A veterinary officer at Koala Town will then conduct the post mortem examination, although Mr Smith believes it might be a case of "pure and simple old age".

Bette had become something of a star in her own right in Brisbane. She was due to appear in this morning's *Burke's Backyard* gardening program on Channel 9.

Mr Smith said he received a message of condolence late yesterday from the "Gold Coast Cane Toad Lovers' Society", whose president, Mrs Lily Frond, said: "All of our hops are with you at this time."

* Bette update: Bette, who died on 30 January 1989, had actually managed to achieve second place inasmuch as Totally Awesome of Iowa had preceded her in going to meet its maker. No mysterious circumstances in this case—simply an inevitable demise due to advanced age.

IMPERSONATE THEM. A visitor on holiday in Queensland was so bewitched by the cane toad spell that it stayed with him after he returned home to Adelaide, where he was arrested for impersonating a toad.

THIRTY-TWO-YEAR-OLD PHILIP WILLIAM ELLIOT WAS CHARGED AFTER HE WAS FOUND CROUCHING ON THE SIDE OF A ROAD AT BIRKENHEAD IN ADELAIDE. POLICE SAY ELLIOT WAS JUMPING OUT ONTO THE ROAD INTO THE PATH OF ONCOMING MOTORCARS. WHEN HE WAS QUESTIONED, HE TOLD THEM HE WAS SIR JOH BJELKE-PETERSEN* AND A CANE TOAD. HE'S PLEADED GUILTY TO A CHARGE OF DISORDERLY BEHAVIOUR AND HAS BEEN FINED $50.

———
—Adelaide radio item
* A former colourful Premier of Queensland.

USE THEM. Brian Hawke, a binding conservator and a tanner at the National Library in Canberra, used cane toad hide to cover a book for the Prince and Princess of Wales.

Queenslanders tried hard to find useful contributions of the cane toad, and these ran the whole spectrum from crummy to grandiose.

Bill Coburn from the Department of Defence asked me could I bind a book for Prince Charles and Lady Di for the wedding present, some-

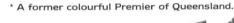

thing very special. I immediately thought: Cane toads! It took about a month to join five, six skins and I emblazoned it with the crest Defence Department. It worked out all right because the Department received a letter from Buckingham Palace. "We are both overwhelmed by your great kindness in thinking of sending us such a splendid wedding present. Thank you so much for taking all the trouble to find something which is so greatly appreciated and will bring so much pleasure to us both throughout our married life. Yours sincerely, Charles."

And in his own hand, "Would you please pass on our warmest thanks to all those who contributed so generously towards this gift. Yours most sincerely, Charles."

—BRIAN HAWKE,
National Library binding conservator and tanner

Some Queenslanders even tried to eke some value out of the poison contained in cane toad skin.

Because of the bufotenine in cane toad skin, alternative uses for it veer towards the bizarre. In Japan this substance is used as an aphrodisiac on the one hand and a hair restorer on the other. In China, it is rumoured to be used in heart operations because it slows down the pulse rate. But there are alternative uses as well.

SMOKE THEM. At the Drug Squad in Brisbane a Heinz baby food jar carries the label *Venom cane toad, hallucinogenic, bufotenine*. Inside the jar is a dry, flaky, crystallized brown substance with an obnoxious odour. The substance is dried toad skins, which naturally include bufotenine. It can be shredded and put into a hookah or a pipe and smoked. It's said to have an intense hallucinatory effect that lasts for several hours.

You use a little qua . . . use a little quantity at first . . . then larger . . . little bit first . . . then . . . Well, er, Don Juan, er, says that er, some of the South American Indians, they, er, when they get the mescaline out of the cactus they say that . . . and have it . . . that you actually start to see the world through the consciousness of the cactus . . . er, you start to see what the world looks like through the eyes of the cactus . . . er, your toad's the same. I am seeing the world . . . er . . . through the consciousness of a toad.

—Cane toad drug abuser

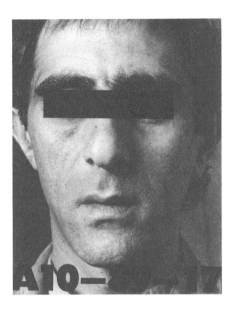

Cane toad poison is a mixture of several compounds and one group of compounds are steroids which affect the heart muscle. They are generally known as *Bufo* toxins or bufotenine—and they are toxins that kill. The glands which produce the toxic material are located in the skin over both shoulder regions, right and left. If you were to press those glands, the venom would shoot out for about a metre (39 inches).

—DR. BOB ENDEAN,
Associate Professor of Zoology, Queensland University

If they couldn't get marijuana or heroin, the next best thing was to go out and get a cane toad. Kill it, boil it down in a tin billy for ten minutes or so, into a solution. It doesn't actually solidify: it's a bit like treacle. They'd spread it on bread and eat it or add a little water and drink the residue. It warps the sense of time and hazes over the mind. It seems to be a different sort of trip than what they got from other drugs. This one gives a sort of burning feeling all over.*

—DETECTIVE INSPECTOR
SYD CHURCHILL,
Cairns Police Department

SWALLOW THEM. Even though, so far as uses go, this seems to be scraping the bottom of the barrel, Queensland police regarded the threat of crazed addicts with so much alarm that bufotenine came to be listed as a dangerous drug in Schedule 2 of Queensland's Drug Misuse Act. The act allows for a maximum penalty of life imprisonment. Death, on the one hand, and life imprisonment, on the other, tend to tarnish any gilded image that cane toads could possibly have retained.

---

* WARNING: Do not attempt this at home. Concentrated cane toad poison can be fatal.

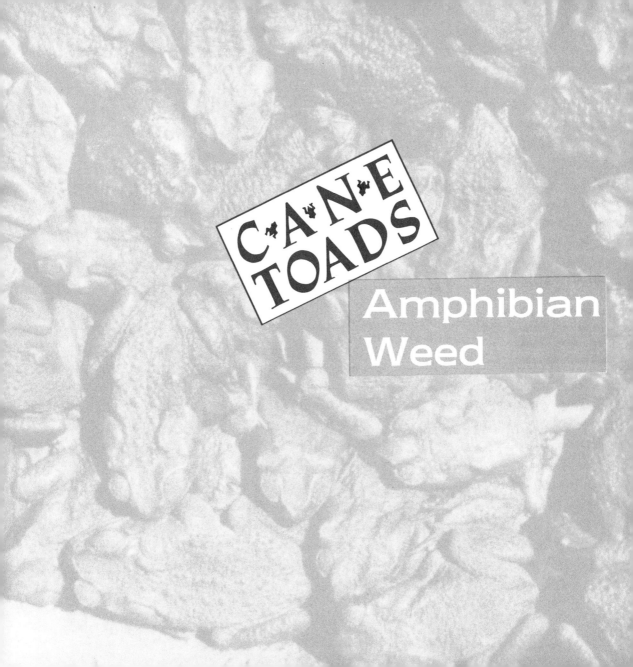

C·A·N·E TOADS

Amphibian Weed

FIVE

Despite its fizzled career and its criminal toxins, the cane toad somehow managed to keep a low profile for about forty years, and during this time it became well established as a successful invader in Australia. In his article "Invasion North" for *Australian Natural History* magazine, Dr. Bill Freeland of the Northern Territory Conservation Commission points out that the cane toad entered an environment in which low rates of parasitism, possibly low rates of predation, and a large under-exploited food supply occur.[1] Each of these made generous contributions to the invading force.

---

[1] Wm. J. Freeland, "Invasion North, Successful Conquest by the Cane Toad," *Australian Natural History*, vol. 22, no. 2 (Spring 1986), p. 72.

An invasion was the last thing expected when Raquel Dexter's speech at the Sugar Cane Technologists' Congress in 1932 swayed the Bureau of Sugar Experiment Stations, but it's not as though the Australians were the only ones who bought it. The toad was introduced into other parts of the world as well, mostly for the same purpose—to control sugarcane beetles. *Bufo* went to Martinique, Barbados, and Jamaica, to islands in the Caribbean, Bermuda, Hawaii, Fiji, the Philippines, Papua New Guinea, and even Egypt.[2] In most places its numbers dwindled or it became extinct. Nowhere else did the toad create as much dissonance as in Australia, nor did it threaten to become a menace.

Could it be Australia? Could the sun be warmer, the rains wetter, the insects more delicious, the fauna more peace-loving? It's almost as though when *Bufo* came to Australia it entered a kind of toad Shangri-la where its zest and well-being achieved heights never before attained.

This potential is what Dr. Freeland suggests when he describes the Australian environment as having low rates of parasitism—so that toads in

The toad is rapidly adapting to conditions that previously might have constrained it. As a result, what we're seeing is the consequence of yet another human-induced ecological disaster in Australia, one in which a single introduced species, the cane toad, is regionally eliminating a

---

[2] Simon Easteal, "The History of Introductions of *Bufo marinus* (Amphibia: Anura); a Natural Experiment in Evolution," *Biological Journal of the Linnean Society*, 1981, pp. 93–113.

Australia are mostly safe from disease—and low rates of predation—because native fauna does not include a species that can cope with toad bufotenine—and a large underexploited food supply— a choice menu of an abundance of insects that are both nourishing and wholesome.

But all this aside, there is yet another aspect of the cane toad that cannot be explained clinically: their ability to know what's best for their survival. It's an intelligent instinct. They anticipate when and where food is left out for dogs or cats and join in the repast without fear or hesitation. They turn a selected shelter spot into a home to which they wend their way and return time and time again— and they choose a particular breeding spot as the customary locale for active sex. Their eyes follow humans about; they know where and when to hide and seem to have a sense of smell. They respond to humans who look after them or pet them or allow contact with them.

They're clever in unexpected ways. Cane toads sit in a circle surrounding streetlights waiting for insects to drop—an easy meal without having to scavenge. Many times cane toads have been seen creating a pyramid—standing on each other's backs to get closer to beehives so they could catch the

host of native animals such as frogs and Australian predators like dasyures and birds. This corruption will have repercussions throughout the whole of the food chain into which the cane toad has insinuated itself. At present we have no way of anticipating the full effects of this disaster. However, at the very least, we can expect some of the native carnivores to undergo severe declines; perhaps even extinctions.
—DR. MICHAEL ARCHER

Comes the wet season in the top end in the world-famous billabongs, you're going to have nothing but a sea of little black tadpoles. In the dry season those famous billabongs are going to be seething with hundreds of thousands of cane toads. From there the total conquest of Northern Australia is but a hop, step and a jump. . . . Hopefully, something can be done prior to the cane toad's invasion of the vast wetlands at the top end of the Northern Territory.

—DR. BILL FREELAND

The biggest problem with toad invasion is aesthetic as opposed to economic. I wouldn't tell people to sell their properties before their real estate value goes down. As the toad

bees at the entrance. This toad tactic made it standard practice for beekeepers in cane toad areas of Queensland to raise their hives off the ground out of reach of the three tiers of cane toads.

It is this uncanny intelligence that is almost a compensation for the toads' total lack of aesthetic beauty. How else to explain why some people relate to these cane toads and find them charismatic? How else to explain why Queenslanders put up with them as they do and accept them?

For about forty years, the cane toad's invasion had been passively accepted. Walter Froggatt's original warnings in 1936 came to a dead end when Reg Mungomery branded him a crank. Why didn't

 78

Mr. Froggatt continue to pursue his crusade? Was he really overcome with humiliation? Why was he so easily vanquished? Why did he not fight back with renewed vigour? Why did he not denounce Reg, treat him as an upstart, and again expose the cane toad as the usurper it has since proven itself to be?

Answers to all these questions hinge on one formidable fact—namely, that for Mr. Froggatt time was running out. When his article denouncing *Bufo* was published in 1936, he was then in his seventy-eighth year. He died the following year, in 1937,* highly respected for his long career as a pioneer Australian naturalist, but, alas, the loser in the controversy surrounding *Bufo*.

Other than Walter Froggatt's concern, there were some brief doubts expressed by J. R. Kinghorn in 1938 which had not been very effective. The aura of calm acceptance prevailed until 1974 when a series of press articles suggested the unlimited spread of the cane toad and pointed to danger signs. Then, inadvertently, the cane toads themselves graphically illustrated these warnings. A

moves in, don't try to stop it, because you can't, anyway. If you're panicking about your children being poisoned by toads, take heart. No one person (in Australia) has died of it yet although dogs and cats can die if they get a good dose of poison. If you're a beekeeper, stick your hives up on stilts. If you're an environmentalist, you have the greatest cause for concern but unfortunately there's not much you can do about it. I think any physical method of stopping the toad from invading won't have much effect. If the toad is coming in, it's coming in.

—DR. ROBERT FLOYD

---

* Proceedings of the Linnean Society of New South Wales, *vol. 67, describes Mr. Froggatt as a dapper fellow: "It was quite unusual to find him without some rare or perfect bloom from his garden in his buttonhole."*

DR. MICHAEL ARCHER

native cat that was a pet of zoologist Michael Archer died in his arms after grasping a cane toad. In another instance, the same Dr. Archer experienced temporary blindness when cane toad toxins were jetted into his eye.

The next year, 1975, saw the first modern study, the work of Jeanette Covacevich of the Queensland Museum, who, with Dr. Archer, researched and documented "The Distribution of the Cane Toad, *Bufo marinus,* in Australia and Its Effects on Indigenous Vertebrates" for *Memoirs of the Queensland Museum.*

Their paper stated that the ranks of the original imported 101 cane toads had swollen to make it the most common small vertebrate in eastern Queensland. They warned that the cane toad is highly toxic and a threat to several native animals, and drew up a list of animals fatally poisoned by attacking or eating cane toads. Snakes such as the red-bellied black snake, the tiger snake, and even death adders are no match for it, they said, as well as kookaburras, native cats, blue-tongued lizards, and scavenging crows. Goannas, too, prized by the Aborigines, are cane toad prey. A first attack had

> We had Kookaburras brought to us at the Queensland Museum with cane toad legs sticking out of their mouths. Halfway through the process of swallowing the cane toad, the Kookaburras simply drop out of the tree—stone dead—as if they had swallowed cyanide pills. The aspect of these discoveries that worried us most was that there was evidently no chance for the native animals to learn about this danger without being killed in the process. A solid bite behind the head of a cane toad gives the native animal no second chance, no warning, no time to avoid a horrible death.
>
> —DR. MICHAEL ARCHER,
> Associate Professor, University of New South Wales

been made and it was heard. Other scientists, too, were becoming intrigued and involved in the cane toad's Australian activity. Among them were Simon Easteal and Dr. Robert Floyd, who were then at the School of Environmental Studies at Griffith University in Queensland. Their work, documented in 1981, was titled "The Cane Toad—An Amphibian Weed"—a weed being something that grows wild and profusely, especially one that grows among cultivated plants and deprives them of space, food, and other necessities.

The toad prefers warm temperatures and a wet

> Only inhabitants of deserts and the frost-prone districts of Australia can afford to relax. The rest of us should be alert for the first signs of these unwelcome visitors. Give Bufo a scrap of encouragement and he'll move right into your backyard.
>
> —GORDON GRIGG, "Bufo the Beastly," *Reader's Digest*, October 1980, p. 86

Just how far it is likely to extend geographically is uncertain. As early as 1936 Mungomery predicted that the range "could possibly extend far into New South Wales coastal districts, until continued severe frosts and cold weather become limiting factors." The presence of *B. marinus* in New South Wales is now a fact and the range in Queensland is extending further west. . . . I would anticipate that *B. marinus* will slowly and progressively increase its geographic range in Queensland, but the real danger lies in toads entering the high rainfall areas of the Northern Territory and northern Western Australia.

—MICHAEL TYLER,
Adelaide University

climate, so it behooves the Northern Territory to be on the alert. With its vast wetlands at the top end, with Kakadu, and all that beautiful *Crocodile Dundee* country—the Northern Territory is a glorious vision, the promised land for cane toads.

The temptation again is to go back to the first attack of Walter Froggatt in 1936, when he had forecast most of the results to be annotated by modern environmentalists from 1974 onwards. Reg Mungomery had then described his criticism as worthless—a statement which could now be challenged. Reg had then added that already *Bufo marinus* was present in the thousands in the northern Queensland cane fields and, moreover, "*Bufo marinus* is now here to stay"—A prophecy that has come true.

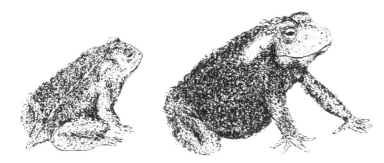

There are now three scientific teams trying to find some means to control of the cane toad. The project materialized because cane toads reached the Northern Territory, where they are breeding up into dense populations—as many as 5,000 around water holes. So far the teams have not made much progress. A virus has been suggested, but now caution guides the action.

No straws are being grasped out of desperation. Australia understands only too well *now* how this can produce effects that are totally unimagined. And where does it all end? Step one: toads against beetles. Step two: virus against toads. Then who knows, but there might even be a step three: something against the virus. Four—five—six—and so on and on.

"Based on the understanding of the thermal physiology of *B. marinus* and the conditions likely to be experienced in nature, climate could limit the distribution of the toad in the following ways. High temperatures could be lethal to embryos and larvae, and low temperatures could prohibit breeding or be lethal to larvae of overwintering toadlets and adults. Since *B. marinus* has such an extensive potential diet, probably has no major predators, and can take advantage of shelter and water around human habitation, its limits of temperature tolerance seem the factors most likely to limit its expanding distribution."[3]

[3] S. EASTEAL and R. B. Floyd, "The Cane Toad—An Amphibian Weed," *Ecology of Exotic Animals and Plants*, School of Environmental Studies, Griffith University, 1986.

If we were going to attempt biological control we might be looking at something like a virus—one that would have a devastating effect on the toad. The danger there, of course, is that if a virus were isolated that affected the cane toad severely, it could [also] affect a whole range of amphibia and maybe even other types of animals and have a devastating effect on them, too.

I don't think we would attempt that in the field until a virus was critically tested in the lab, because there are so many species of frogs, toads, lizards, some of them extremely valuable biologically in this area, and we wouldn't want to put them at risk.

PROFESSOR
ROD CAMPBELL,
Tropical Veterinary Science
Department, James Cook
University

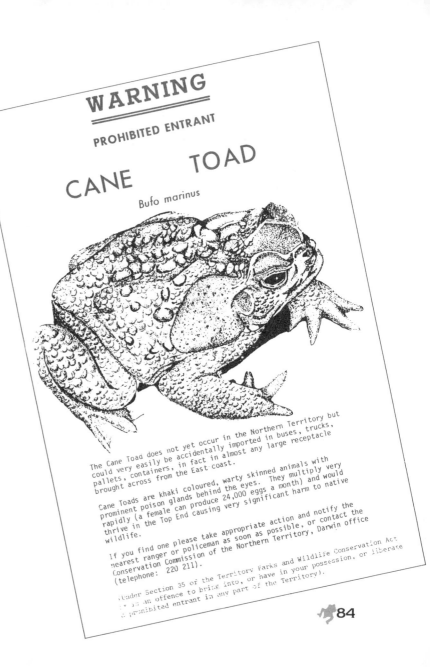

WARNING

PROHIBITED ENTRANT

CANE TOAD

Bufo marinus

The Cane Toad does not yet occur in the Northern Territory but could very easily be accidentally imported in buses, trucks, pallets, containers, in fact in almost any large receptacle brought across from the East coast.

Cane Toads are khaki coloured, warty skinned animals with prominent poison glands behind the eyes. They multiply very rapidly (a female can produce 24,000 eggs a month) and would thrive in the Top End causing very significant harm to native wildlife.

If you find one please take appropriate action and notify the nearest ranger or policeman as soon as possible, or contact the Conservation Commission of the Northern Territory, Darwin office (telephone: 220 211).

(Under Section 35 of the Territory Parks and Wildlife Conservation Act it is an offence to bring into, or have in your possession, or liberate a prohibited entrant in any part of the Territory).

84

He's as big a menace as the German Army was in World War Two. I appeal to everybody—wherever you see a toad, don't hesitate. Run over the monster and kill it.

—TIP BYRNE

When Tip's wife, Noelene, sent this photo, she wrote, "At long last, as requested, the photo of Queensland's most promising film star."

I line them up with the driver's side front wheel. It's not quite as easy as it used to be with the big fat tyres on the RX4 Mazda,* but I seem to be able to get most of the ones I line up on the right-hand side of the road. I know I've made a clean kill, particularly if the toad is actually facing towards the vehicle, because the air that's inside the toad is trapped within the head and blown out towards the back end and the toad goes off with a bang—like a balloon going off. I have a profound love of the natural wildlife around here. So if it was possible to remove cane toads and totally eradicate them—and I was capable of doing it—I would spend a lifetime doing exactly that.

—BRENT VINCENT
Cairns resident

_____

* Mr. Vincent now drives a Volkswagen Kombi-Van.

So it appears there is no weapon that can successfully thwart the cane toads' invasion as yet ... but Queensland, Australia, and the world's wetlands remain hopeful.

Even Tip Byrne now has changed his tune. He has succumbed to contemplations on murder and makes an appeal to motor car drivers to assume the role of executioner.

A University of Queensland undergraduate has estimated that 200 tonnes (220 tons) of cane toad flesh is squelched into Queensland roads every year. On a damp night, with a bit of rain, the roads can be covered with dead cane toads flattened by motorcars. The stench is said to be as noxious as a swarm of mullets coming up the river.

MERINGA GRUB STATION

SIX

 Mr. A. J. Hesp, writing for the Mulgrave Shire Historical Society, reported that in 1947 Jim Buzacott, who had been Reg Mungomery's partner at the Grub Station in Meringa when they were both young men, led the team that introduced benzene hexachloride (B.H.C. or Gammexane) into the sugarcane fields. This substance finally succeeded in keeping the cane grubs under control. Its use is credited with the economic survival of the sugar industry and it won the M.B.E. for Jim.[1]

---

[1] A. J. Hesp, *Mulgrave Shire Historical Society*, Bulletin no. 64, February 1984.

Right throughout the ages toads have had the reputation of being associated with some form of evil. Consequently, it's not surprising that whenever this toad becomes established in a new area most people there should regard it with suspicion, repulsion, and even fear, for, unfortunately, its rather ugly appearance does nothing to enhance its sinister reputation. Some of the stories told about toads, therefore, are coloured by fiction, rather than by fact. . . . Though, no doubt, *Bufo* will continue to be maligned in many quarters, it is certain that if he is given a fair trial, the scales of justice will weigh heavily in his favour.

—REG MUNGOMERY,
1949 speech for the Australian
Broadcasting Commission

Two years later, in 1949, fourteen years after he'd brought the toads from Hawaii in two cases, nurtured and pampered them, and succeeded in getting them to breed in captivity, Reg Mungomery was still defending his stand on cane toads.

Reg passed away in 1972. His obituary in the *Cane Growers' Quarterly* makes no mention of his starring role in the cane toad drama.

Today, there are still survivors of the time of the cane toad introduction. Graham Hughes, George Wilson, and Tom Edgerton still feel kindly about the toad and refuse to be ruffled by the scientists' reports. Their general attitude seems to be that all this newfangled nonsense could be a kind of mild hysteria.

George Wilson is eighty-two years old. In 1935 he was the chap who delivered toadlets in beer bottles and kerosene tins soon after the original introduction. He feels the toads aren't the problem.

And what about the sugar growers—the disillusioned grower who had originally clamoured for and waited impatiently for the toad because he'd been led to believe it would be the saviour of the sugar cane?

In 1935 the cane growers really didn't know what to do about the cane beetles. And now nobody really knows what to do about the cane toad— what to make of it, what to do with it, or even how to think about it.

Right from the beginning, the circumstances surrounding the toad involved a gnashing of teeth and a clutching at straws. One overreaction spurred another. Money was involved—politics, too. And

I think human beings are very much greater danger to the fauna than the toads are. I think it's just a waste of money to try and stop them. There's no need to wipe out the cane toad in the first place and I don't think there's any practical way they could. The idea that they can investigate how to control the cane toads between here and the Northern Territory is just utter nonsense. If they try to do anything, it's just a waste of money, because from my experience of the way the cane toad can produce and spread, they're not in the race.

—GEORGE WILSON

Well, as I said, my dad was an Irishman, but this time he was *wrong*. The cane toad didn't have the grub by the balls—it had *us* by the balls. You know, looking back over the years and so forth, when you look at our imports, what we brought into Australia, this must have been a great country long before white men ever came to the joint. We brought in foxes and hares and then, to cap it all off, we bring in this monstrous thing called a toad.

—TIP BYRNE

desperation, pathos, warnings, and loyalties all came into play somewhere along the line.

Well-meaning human frailty engaged in a head-on collision with a thick-skinned, insensitive creature whose great talent—nay, genius—lies in its innate ability to breed, proliferate . . .

and to stay.

Cast of Characters

Ackland, Max, Councillor of the Mulgrave Shire.

Archer, Dr. Michael, Associate Professor Zoology, University of New South Wales.

Bell, Arthur F., entomologist and deputy director of the Bureau of Sugar Experiment Stations in the 1930s and official Queensland delegate to the Sugar Cane Technologists' Congress in Puerto Rico in 1932.

Brody, Dr. Janos, resident medical officer of the Mulgrave Shire in 1941 in Gordonvale.

Buzacott, James Hardie, the other half of the two-man team with Reg Mungomery at the Meringa

Station in 1935, the time of the toad introduction.

Buzacott, Jim, Jr., Gordonvale resident.

Byrne, Tip, whose father had a sugarcane farm at Tully in the 1930s.

Campbell, Professor R., Tropical Veterinary Science Department, James Cook University, Townsville.

Churchill, Syd, Detective Inspector with the Cairns Police Department.

Clark, Jack, cane farmer at Gordonvale since the 1930s.

Connolly, Gerry, former altar boy.

Cook, Patrick, social commentator and cartoonist.

Covacevich, Jeanette, curator of reptiles, Queensland Museum.

Dalton, Bettina, ranger with the Queensland National Parks and Wildlife Service.

Dexter, Raquel, entomologist who gave a paper at the San Juan, Puerto Rico, Congress of the International Society of Sugar Cane Technologists in 1932.

Easteal, Simon, Biology Department, Australian National University, Canberra, A.C.T.

Edgerton, Tom, member of the Cane Pest Board at the time of the toad introduction.

> You've got to live through some of that stuff just to see what it's like. Those greyback beetles—they flew and they flew. They flew into your house at night. They were there literally in the millions and millions. And to try and control them by any method whatsoever was an extraordinary proposal.
>
> —JACK CLARK

 96

Elliot, Philip William, toad impersonator.

Endean, Dr. Robert, Associate Professor of Zoology, Queensland University.

Floyd, Dr. Robert, animal ecologist who had been on the C.S.I.R.O. staff and at Griffith University.

Freeland, Dr. Bill, Northern Territory Conservation Commission.

Froggatt, Walter W., president of the New South Wales Naturalist Society, 1935–36, and first objector to the toad introduction.

Greig, Elvie, Redcliffe resident and friend of the toads.

Grigg, Gordon, Zoology Department, University of Queensland.

Hawke, Brian, binding conservator, National Library, Canberra, A.C.T.

Hughes, Graham, member of the Meringa Station original entomological team that introduced the toad in 1935.

Ingram, Dr. Glen, senior curator, amphibia and birds, Queensland Museum.

Kraus, Peter, cane toad exporter.

Kreuger, John, Townsville toad taxidermist.

Monica, Dairy Queen's keeper.

Mungomery, R. W. (Reg), entomologist at the Meringa Sugar Experiment Station with partner,

Prior to the introduction, the bugs and beetles and insects were so thick that it was unpleasant to sit and have a game of cards at night or ride a bike down the road. After the toad took over the air was as clean as in this room. The mosquitoes used to be like a cloud around you. Today you'd hardly see a mozzie. I put that down to what the toad did up in the North. He's not as bad as they make out. Just take one up and have a look in its eyes—a lovely pair of eyes.

—TOM EDGERTON, member of the Cane Pest Board at the time of the introduction of the cane toads

Jim Buzacott, at the time of the toad introduction.

Pemberton, Cyril, executive entomologist with the Hawaiian Sugar Planters Association Experiment Station at the time of the toad introduction.

Pitt, Warren, Gordonvale Chamber of Commerce.

Prien, Bill, Senior Vice President, Gordonvale Chamber of Commerce.

Roth, Marie, Gordonvale resident.

Sondergard, Dave, Cairns resident.

Straughan, I. R., formerly of the Zoology Department, University College of Townsville, Queensland.

Traynor, Maurie, Palmwood resident.

Tyler, Michael, reader in zoology, Adelaide University.

Vincent, Brent, Cairns resident.

White, Patrick, old-time Gordonvale farmer.

Wilhoft, Daniel, American Fulbright scholar in Australia in the 1960s.

Wilson, George, member of the South Johnstone Cane Pest Destruction Board at the time of the toad introduction.

Cane toads are coming, cane toads are coming,
Main roads are humming with the cane toad blues,
Cane toads are coming, cane toads are coming,
Main roads are humming with the cane toad blues.
Cane toads . . .
When are you gonna leave me alone?
Heading south,
Like a case of foot and mouth
Cane toads . . .
You're supposed to set us free
Yeah, yeah, yeah.

Cane toads are coming, cane toads are coming . . .
Main roads are humming with the cane toad blues
Cane toads are coming, cane toads are coming,
Main roads are humming with the cane toad blues.
Cane toads
ba, pa, da . . .
da, pa, da, pa, da, da, da,

Cane toads
You go chomp and live in the swamp
Yeah.
Cane toads,
You're supposed to set us free
Yeah, yeah, yeah, yeah.

Cane toads are coming,
Main roads are humming with the cane toad blues.
Cane toads are coming, cane toads are coming,
Main roads are humming with the cane toad blues.
Yeah . . . . (whistles . . .)

Words and music © 1988 Tim Finn

Stephanie Lewis, a former New Yorker, began her career with dispatches and stories from New Guinea for the American Red Cross during World War II. After the war, she was Chief Staff Writer for WTOP radio, a CBS affiliate. Stephanie has acted in summer stock theater and in a mini-series, and studied art in Florence, Italy. As a pioneer rural Australian wife, her role was fraught with bushfires, floods, and two sons. More recently, she is a contributing journalist and book editor for tertiary education books.

Mark Lewis, a graduate of Sydney University and the Australian Film and Television School, is now a writer and director. His latest film, *Cane Toads,* gained worldwide notoriety and provided the inspiration for *Cane Toads,* the book. Mark's future projects include several dramas and another *Cane Toads*—style documentary entitled *The Wonderful World of Dogs.*

BOOKMARK

This book was set in the typefaces Sabon and Newtext by
the Monotype Composition Company, Baltimore,
Maryland.
It was printed on Finch, an acid-free paper, by Arcata,
Halliday, West Hanover, Massachusetts.

Designed by Marysarah Quinn